Our Appointment with Life

The Essential Sutra Trilogy

Through decades of teaching, Zen Master Thích Nhất Hạnh identified three sutras as central to meditation practice: the Sutra on the Full Awareness of Breathing, the Sutra on the Four Establishments of Mindfulness, and the Sutra on Knowing the Better Way to Live Alone. Among his earliest books published in English were his three commentaries on these sutras—*Breathe, You Are Alive!*, *Transformation and Healing*, and *Our Appointment with Life*—which he advised his students to keep by their side and study regularly. They continue to be essential reading for meditators today.

First published in 1990 by Parallax Press, these books now offer introductions and additional commentaries by a new generation of teachers in Thích Nhất Hạnh's lineage, inviting us to apply the timeless wisdom of these sutras to modern life.

Our Appointment with Life

SUTRA ON KNOWING
THE BETTER WAY TO LIVE ALONE

THICH NHAT HANH

Foreword by Brother Pháp Linh

Parallax Press

BERKELEY, CALIFORNIA

Parallax Press
P.O. Box 7355
Berkeley, California 94707
parallax.org

Parallax Press is the publishing division of
Plum Village Community of Engaged Buddhism, Inc.

Cover design by Katie Eberle
Interior design by Maureen Forys
Cover photography by Yudo Kurita

Foreword adapted from a Dharma talk given on
November 22, 2018, in the Assembly of Stars Meditation Hall,
Lower Hamlet, Plum Village, France.

Printed in the United States of America by Versa
Printed on FSC-certified paper

Parallax Press's authorized representative in the EU
and the EEA is SAS Plum Village at Home Point UH,
437 Chemin du Pey, Thénac, France
Email: europe@parallax.org

ISBN 978-1-967175-08-6
Ebook ISBN 978-1-967175-10-9

LCCN 2026942211

1 2 3 4 5 VERSA 30 29 28 27 26

MIX
Paper | Supporting
responsible forestry
FSC® C005010

Contents

Our appointment with life is
in the present moment.
The place of our appointment is
right here, in this very place.

—THÍCH NHẤT HẠNH

Foreword

The Better Way to Time Travel

IN THE 1980S, neuroscientists got very excited about a machine called a positron emission tomography (PET) scanner, which had been developed in the late 1960s. PET scanners use radioactive tracers to measure metabolic activity in the brain, allowing scientists to localize brain activity in three dimensions over the course of a few minutes. With this machine, scientists hoped to correlate parts of the brain with different functions such as language processing, memory, and problem solving. What they actually found, however, was unexpected. When they asked someone to go into the scanner and perform any kind of mental task—to remember a set of words, for instance—many different parts of the brain became activated, not just one. They weren't able to localize functions as they'd hoped.

So the scientists decided to establish a control; they hypothesized that if they could get a snapshot of the brain's activity while it was "doing nothing," and subtract that from the "on task" scan, then whichever areas still showed activity on the resulting image must be those engaged with the task. And they made the fairly reasonable assumption that the "doing nothing" scan would detect less activity than the "on task" scan. But once again, their expectations were confounded; when participants lay in the scanner and "did nothing," their brains became even more active than before.

A few years later, a PhD student named Nancy Andreasen performed a groundbreaking study on this so-called "resting state." She asked people to go into the PET scanner, do nothing, and report back on what happened. What, in actuality, was their conscious experience of doing nothing really like? Almost all participants reported daydreaming while lying in the PET scanner: they thought about something in the future, maybe something they needed to do in the next few days, or about the past, whether recent or distant. Without any particular conscious intent, their minds zipped back and forth between past and future, over and over—a familiar experience for us all.

The part of the brain that becomes active when we're apparently "doing nothing" has since been named the "default mode network." Scientists have performed thousands of studies on the default mode network, and some even take it to be what distinguishes humans from all other animals. According to them, the ability it underwrites—which they call "mental time travel"—is unique to humanity. (It's worth noting, though, that this type of claim doesn't tend to age well.)

It's precisely this "mental time travel" that some meditation skeptics believe will be suppressed by mindfulness practice. They think that to practice mindfulness is to zone out, to ignore the past and future completely, and therefore to weaken our capacity for reflection and foresight. They think that when we are stranded in the la-la land of the present moment, we're unable to learn from earlier events or make plans, and our ability to live safe, productive, and creative lives slips away.

Being at One

The Sutra on the Better Way to Live Alone deals directly with the issue of our relationship to the past, the present, and the future.

In Pali, the language in which the teachings of the Buddha were first set down, it is called the Bhaddekaratta Sutta. As Thầy Thích Nhất Hạnh explains in this book,* "Bhaddekaratta" is a compound of *bhadda* (best, ideal), *eka* (one), and *ratta* (to enjoy, to appreciate). By translating *eka* as "alone," Thầy is not suggesting that the Buddha recommends being physically alone. Instead, Thầy is highlighting the Buddha's invitation to enjoy being at one with ourselves, and not internally divided and scattered by past regrets, anxious imaginings, or compulsive thoughts and cravings.

With mindfulness, we start to notice when we are dwelling in regrets about the past or hopes and dreams about the future. When such thoughts arise, I find it helpful to ask, "With this thought, am I really alone?" Zooming involuntarily back and forth between the past and the future I notice how much my thinking and feeling is guided by how I think others see me. I am propelled into the past and the future

* *Thầy is an affectionate Vietnamese term for teacher (eds.).*

by rehearsing interactions mostly with those whose opinion really matters to me or with whom there is tension—and of course, those can often be the same person.

And as I rehash past interactions and imagine future encounters, I find that they are all there with me, in my head. We may be learning from the past and planning for the future in these moments, but it's worth paying close attention to the felt experience of this rumination, to discover how much it is colored by anxiety, worry, or regret. What does the Buddha advise doing to avoid this pervasive background worrying? Does he recommend ignoring the past and the future altogether? Looking to the sutra for an answer, we find the lines: "Do not pursue the past. Do not lose yourself in the future." The Buddha goes on to explain this teaching in detail:

> Friends, what do we mean by "pursuing the past"? When someone considers the way their body was in the past, the way their feelings were in the past, the way their perceptions were in the past, the way their mental formations were in the past, the way their consciousness was in the past; when they consider these things and their mind is burdened by and attached to these things which belong to the past, then that person is pursuing the past.

The Buddha applies similar criteria to determine if we're "losing ourselves in the future":

> When someone considers the way their body will be in the future, the way their feelings will be in the future . . . when

> they consider these things and their mind is burdened by and daydreaming about these things which belong to the future, then that person is losing themselves in the future.

In both cases, the Buddha offers a test we can apply: "Am I attached to this experience of the past? Am I burdened by this experience of the future? Is it dragging me down? Or am I contemplating the past, contemplating the future, in stability and freedom?"

It's important not to take the Buddha's instruction as a moral judgment; this isn't a matter of right or wrong, good or bad. It's not about whether we should or shouldn't think of the future or the past, it's about the way. The Buddha invites us to notice that there are two ways to think about the past, and two ways to think about the future. In each case, one makes us feel bad. All he's saying is, "If it's making you suffer, then don't do it like that."

But the Buddha doesn't explain how to "not do it like that." We must discover for ourselves the root cause—the thing that gives our thinking about the past or the future its pervasive anxious quality. Only then will we be able to visit the past and the future with solidity and freedom. No longer chased by the ghosts of past regrets, or haunted by fears for the future, we will find ourselves at one. Leaving the self-conscious hall of mirrors of all our imagined relationships, we will discover the true meaning of being "alone."

Who Are We Really?

I have mentioned four ways of being in time described by the Buddha: pursuing the past, not pursuing the past, losing ourselves in the future, and not losing ourselves in the future. According to the Buddha, there are two more: we can also be swept away by the present moment, or not.

In the case of the present moment, the Buddha highlights the problem of identification with the five aggregates or skandhas: the experiences of body, feelings, perceptions, mental formations, and consciousness. He invites us to check if, in the present moment, there is an unconscious conviction operating in the background: "I am this body, these feelings, these thoughts, perceptions, and consciousness; these five things are me." Because whenever we identify with the skandhas, we are consolidating the idea that we genuinely exist as a separate entity—a self.

These, then, are the two ways to be in the present: to experience the present through the lens of self or not through the lens of self. The Buddha recommends the second option, and the reason is clear: Experiencing life through the lens of self automatically entails anxiety, lack, fear, and desire—or, simply, suffering.

To dwell in the present—in freedom, then—is simply to not give rise to the thought, "This body is me; these feelings are me; this thinking, these perceptions, and this consciousness are me." But, again, he doesn't explain how. So we may be left feeling a bit stranded: "How do I not give rise to a thought?" But also, "If I'm not my body, my feelings, my thoughts, perceptions and consciousness, then who am I? These are both excellent questions for meditation.

The Buddha is encouraging us to look carefully into our own experience and see that where we assume something solid and separate—a self—there is only interconnectedness; as Thầy puts it, there is only interbeing. We are not separate from our parents, teachers, our friends, or our society. The whole of life—across time and space—flows through us in each moment. But it is one thing to agree with that conceptually and quite another to experience it directly.

The Inexplicable Present

The Buddha reminds us that the past, the future—any experience of life—is only available in the here and now. But do we truly know what it's like to be in the present moment?

I've found that as soon as I think I've understood the present moment, the door to life closes, and I'm stuck again in the realm of notions. So I try not to know what the present moment is. In fact, I prefer to assume that I haven't even experienced it yet. Because then my mind is open, and my curiosity is engaged.

After all, the present moment may be fundamentally inexplicable. And that would be good news, because then the present—the beating heart of life—will remain a mystery. It's also why we must resist the urge to explain it away. If we grab ahold of that mysterious quality, pin it down with language and concepts, and claim we've explained it, all we've done is distance ourselves still further from life. The fact that we can't explain the present moment doesn't mean we can't experience it. Indeed, letting go of what we think we know about the present moment—unknowing it—may be the only way to truly touch it.

This is the depth of reality the Buddha invites us to explore with this sutra. With Thầy's commentary as our gentle guide, and with ease and boundless curiosity, may we settle ever deeper into the ungraspable experience of the now.

—Brother Pháp Linh
Plum Village, France

Introduction

What Does It Mean to Live Alone?

The Sutra on Knowing the Better Way to Live Alone is called the Bhaddekaratta Sutta in Pali. It is number 131 in the Majjhima Nikāya. This important sutra is one of the oldest written teachings on how to live in the present moment.

"Knowing how to live alone" doesn't mean you have to live in solitude in a cave, separated from other people. If we sit alone in a cave, lost in our thinking, we aren't really living alone. "Living alone" means living to have sovereignty over ourselves, to have the freedom that comes from not being dragged away by the past, not living in fear of the future, and not being pulled around by strong emotions caused by the circumstances of the present. When we are master of ourselves, we can grasp the situation as it is, and we're in the best position to handle whatever may arise. When we dwell in mindfulness day and night, then we are truly practicing "the better way to live alone." This is true whether we are surrounded by friends and family, or when we are living a solitary life.

If a doctor tells you, "You have cancer and probably only have six months to live," you will likely feel completely overwhelmed. The fear, the idea that "I'm going to die in six months," can take away your peace and joy. Before the doctor told you about the cancer you could sit and enjoy your tea, eat your meal, or watch the moon, while now your fear takes away all your joy and freedom.

But the doctor's words can be a bell of mindfulness. We all have six months left to live, or seven months, or ten years. If we can know and accept that death is something that comes to everybody, we will not suffer so much. The doctor who tells us we have six months left to live will also die. Maybe the doctor will die before us. We may be lucky to have six months to live. If we look deeply, we see things that we can't otherwise see. We can get back our freedom from fear and, with that freedom and non-fear, we may live those six months happily.

We are all equal as far as life and death are concerned. Everyone has to die. But before we die, can we live properly? If we live properly, the quality of our last six months can be higher than if we were to live six or sixty more years. If we're caught in the fetters of suffering, our life doesn't have the same meaning it would if we lived in freedom. Knowing that we have to die, we can become determined to live our lives properly and deeply. If we're not able to live with peace, joy, and freedom, then we live as if we're already dead.

In the Sutra on Knowing the Better Way to Live Alone, the Buddha teaches that we must struggle to get back our freedom, to be able to live the moments of our daily life deeply. If in the moments of our daily life we can have peace and joy, then we can heal the suffering we have in our bodies and our minds. Living deeply in each moment of our life we can be in touch with the wonderful things of life; we can nourish our body and mind with these wonderful elements, and we can embrace and transform our suffering. To live each day of our life deeply is to live a life of wonder, nourishment, and healing. Living like this we can revive our freedom, experience life deeply, give rise to the truth, and have awakened understanding. Our fears, anxieties, sufferings, and sadness will evaporate, and we will become a source of joy and life for ourselves and those around us.

Living Alone in the Present Moment

There are people who can't see the happiness of the present and think that life was more beautiful in the past. Many of us are caught in this way of thinking. The past is no longer there, but we compare it with the present. Even when we were living those moments in the past we didn't really value them at the time, because in the past we also weren't able to live in the present moment.

There are other people who pursue the past because the past made them suffer. We have all suffered in the past, and those heavy wounds are calling us back: "Come back to the past. You cannot escape me." We can become like sheep running back to the past for it to enclose and imprison us, and make us suffer.

Sometimes when we're sitting with a friend, we can feel abandoned by that friend, because our friend is drowning in the past. They are sitting next to us, but they're not really there. Suppose we find a way to free our friend from the past. We might ask them what they are thinking, or touch them gently in some way to remind them of the present moment. Then our friend may wake up and smile, and be free from the prison of the past.

Sometimes we don't want to go back into the past, but the past grabs hold of us and pulls us back. We have to look directly into the past, smile at it and say, "You can no longer oppress me. I am free of you." The past is just a ghost. We know that the past is a ghost, but we allow the ghost to imprison us.

Some of us run to pursue the future. But the future is another ghost. Why are we afraid of the future? Fear comes from our worry that this or that will or won't happen tomorrow. But the future is something that is not yet here. The future is never here. Once it's here, it's the present.

When we live with a ghost we're not living alone, we're living with another. We eat a meal, but we have the ghost sitting alongside us. When we see a friend sitting with a ghost we can say, "Who are you sitting with?" and perhaps that person will wake up. It's not just the ghosts of the past and the future that like to sit with us. In the present we have infatuations, attachments, feelings of sadness, and projects that take us away from the joy of the present moment. When we live with these things, we are not living alone; we are living with ghosts.

The ghosts of the past and the future take away a lot of our freedom. We can become their slaves. They follow us and condition our life, and order us about. But if we know how to deal with them, we will never fall under their influence. We only have to smile at them. We only need to breathe and come back to our awareness of the present moment and say, "Oh, I know you are a ghost."

Being aware in the present moment does not preclude our thinking about the past or the future. But we must still dwell in the present moment whenever we look deeply into the past or the future, so that we can be aware of any fear or sadness without being overwhelmed by it. According to the teachings of interbeing, the past makes the present, and the present makes the future. Being in touch with the present, we are already in touch with the past and the future.

We're caught by the ghosts of the past and the future because we don't know they're ghosts. We think the past is still right here with us, and we dwell in it. But if we can smile to the ghost of the past, and acknowledge that the past was there, but that now it is gone, then we can have the smile of enlightenment. When we smile like that, it shows we have love for ourselves. We know the past and the future are not our enemies. We know how to live in this moment we are in right now. We need to live our daily moments deeply, as they occur. When we live and know that we are living, this is freedom.

The Sutras

The Elder Sutra*

I HEARD THESE WORDS of the Buddha one time when the Lord was staying at the monastery in the Jeta Grove, in the town of Shravasti. At that time there was a monk named Thera (Elder), who always preferred to be alone. Whenever he could, he praised the practice of living alone. He sought alms alone and sat in meditation alone.

One time a group of bhikshus came to the Lord. They paid their respect by prostrating at his feet, stepped to one side, sat down at a distance, and said, "Blessed One, there is an elder by the name of Thera who only wants to be alone. He always praises the practice of living alone. He goes into the village alone to seek alms, returns home from the village alone, and sits in meditation alone."

The Lord Buddha told one of the bhikshus, "Please go to the place where the monk Thera lives and tell him I wish to see him."

The bhikshu obeyed. When the monk Thera heard the Buddha's wish he came without delay, prostrated at the feet of the

* *Samyukta Agama 1071. The equivalent in the Pali Canon is the Theranamo Sutta (Samyutta Nikāya, Sutta number 10). This version is translated from the Chinese by Thich Nhat Hanh.*

Buddha, stepped to one side, and sat down at a distance. Then the Blessed One asked the monk Thera, "Is it true that you prefer to be alone, praise the life of solitude, go for alms alone, come back from the village alone, and sit in meditation alone?"

The monk Thera replied, "It is true, Blessed One." Buddha asked the monk Thera, "How do you live alone?"

The monk Thera replied, "I live alone; no one else lives with me. I praise the practice of being alone. I go for alms alone, and I come back from the village alone. I sit in meditation alone. That is all."

The Buddha taught the monk as follows. "It is obvious that you like the practice of living alone. I do not want to deny that, but I want to tell you that there is a more wonderful and profound way to be alone. It is the way of deep observation to see that the past no longer exists and the future has not yet come, and to dwell at ease in the present moment, free from desire. When a person lives in this way, they have no hesitation in their heart. They give up all anxieties and regrets, let go of all binding desires, and cut the fetters which prevent them from being free. This is called 'the better way to live alone.' There is no more wonderful way of being alone than this."

Then the Blessed One recited this gatha:

Observing life deeply,
it is possible to see clearly all that is.
Not enslaved by anything,
it is possible to put aside all craving,

resulting in a life of peace and joy.
This is truly to live alone.

Hearing the Lord's words, the monk Thera was delighted. He prostrated respectfully to the Buddha and departed.

The Sutra on Knowing the Better Way to Live Alone*

I HEARD THESE WORDS of the Buddha one time when the Lord was staying at the monastery in the Jeta Grove, in the town of Shravasti. He called all the monks to him and instructed them, "Bhikkhus!"†

And the bhikkhus replied, "We are here."

The Blessed One taught, "I will teach you what is meant by 'knowing the better way to live alone.' I will begin with an outline of the teaching, and then I will give a detailed explanation. Bhikkhus, please listen carefully."

"Blessed One, we are listening."

The Buddha taught:

"Do not pursue the past.
Do not lose yourself in the future.
The past no longer is.

* *The Bhaddekaratta Sutta (Majjhima Nikāya, Sutta number 131). This version is translated from the Pali by Thich Nhat Hanh.*

† Bhikkhu *is the Pali equivalent of the Sanskrit word* bhikshu.

The future has not yet come.
Looking deeply at life as it is
in the very here and now,
the practitioner dwells
in stability and freedom.
We must be diligent today.
To wait till tomorrow is too late.
Death comes unexpectedly.
How can we bargain with it?
The sage calls a person who
dwells in mindfulness
night and day
'the one who knows
the better way to live alone.'

"Bhikkhus, what do we mean by 'pursuing the past'? When someone considers the way their body was in the past, the way their feelings were in the past, the way their perceptions were in the past, the way their mental formations were in the past, the way their consciousness was in the past; when they consider these things and their mind is burdened by and attached to these things which belong to the past, then that person is pursuing the past.

"Bhikkhus, what is meant by 'not pursuing the past'? When someone considers the way their body was in the past, the way their feelings were in the past, the way their perceptions were in the past, the way their mental formations were in the past, the way their consciousness was in the past; when they consider these things but their mind is neither enslaved by nor attached to these things which belong to the past, then that person is not pursuing the past.

"Bhikkhus, what is meant by 'losing yourself in the future'? When someone considers the way their body will be in the future, the way their feelings will be in the future, the way their perceptions will be in the future, the way their mental formations will be in the future, the way their consciousness will be in the future; when they consider these things and their mind is burdened by and daydreaming about these things which belong to the future, then that person is losing themselves in the future.

"Bhikkhus, what is meant by 'not losing yourself in the future'? When someone considers the way their body will be in the future, the way their feelings will be in the future, the way their perceptions will be in the future, the way their mental formations will be in the future, the way their consciousness will be in the future; when they consider these things but their mind is not burdened by or daydreaming about these things which belong to the future, then they are not losing themselves in the future.

"Bhikkhus, what is meant by 'being swept away by the present'? When someone does not study or learn anything about the Awakened one, or the teachings of love and understanding, or the community that lives in harmony and awareness, when that person knows nothing about the noble teachers and their teachings, does not practice these teachings, and thinks, 'This body is myself, I am this body; these feelings are myself, I am these feelings; this perception is myself, I am this perception; this mental formation is myself, I am this mental formation; this consciousness is myself, I am this consciousness,' then that person is being swept away by the present.

"Bhikkhus, what is meant by 'not being swept away by the present'? When someone studies and learns about the Awakened One, the teachings of love and understanding, and the community that lives in harmony and awareness, when that person knows about noble teachers and their teachings, practices these teachings, and does not think, 'This body is myself, I am this body; these feelings are myself, I am these feelings; this perception is myself, I am this perception; this mental formation is myself, I am this mental formation; this consciousness is myself, I am this consciousness,' then that person is not being swept away by the present.

"Bhikkhus, I have presented the outline and the detailed explanation of knowing the better way to live alone."

Thus the Buddha taught, and the bhikkhus were delighted to put his teachings into practice.

Commentary on the Sutras

DURING THE TIME OF THE BUDDHA, there was a bhikkhu named Ekavihariya, who liked to live alone. Literally, his name means "One" (*eka*) "Living" (*vihariya*). The Buddha once praised him with this short gatha that appears in the Dhammapada:

> *Sitting alone, resting alone,*
> *going forth alone, without laziness;*
> *he who understands deeply*
> *the roots of suffering*
> *enjoys great peace,*
> *while dwelling in solitude.*

The monk Ekavihariya was well loved and respected by his fellow practitioners.* There was another monk, named Thera (Elder), who also liked to live alone and often spoke highly of the solitary life. However this monk was not praised by his fellow practitioners or by the Buddha. Perhaps Thera wanted to emulate other solitary monks, or perhaps he just wanted to practice living alone. But he lived the solitary life only according to the outer form, and his fellow practitioners noticed there was something unbalanced about it. They told the Buddha about him, and the Buddha invited Thera to come see him. The Elder Sutra comes from that encounter.

When Thera presented himself, the Buddha questioned him about his daily life and then offered to show him a much

* *Some gathas written by him can be found in the Theragatha (Poems of the Elder Monks), verses 537–546. In these poems he praises the tranquility of living alone.*

more enjoyable way to live alone, a way that was much more deep and wonderful.

Then the Buddha taught him, "Let go of what is past. Let go of what is not yet. Observe deeply what is happening in the present moment, but do not be attached to it. This is the most wonderful way to live alone."*

The title of the sutra in Pali, Theranamo, means "The One Named Thera." It is possible that after the Buddha taught Thera the contents of this sutra, the other monks, out of respect for him, began to refer to him in the sutra as the Elder, rather than by his prior name.

As the Buddha taught, a person who knows the better way to live alone does not necessarily live isolated from society. To put society at a distance and to live isolated in the forest is no guarantee of being alone. When we are surrounded by the past, worries about the future, or distractions of the present, our vision is muddled and we are never alone. One who knows the better way to live alone can see clearly, even in a crowd of people.

The Buddha discussed the importance of living alone in many sutras, including Migajala Sutra.† In this sutra, a monk named Migajala had heard about the teaching of the better way to live alone and came to ask the Buddha about it.

* *This conversation, so similar to the one in Samyukta Agama 1071, is from the Theranamo Sutta, Samyutta Nikāya, Sutta number 10.*

† *From the Samyutta Nikāya, Sutta numbers 63 and 64.*

The Buddha instructed Migajala, "The forms and images which are the objects of our vision can be pleasant, enjoyable, and memorable, and can lead to craving and desire. If a monk is attached to them, then he is bound by them, and he is not alone. He is always with another."

The expression "being with another" is translated from the Pali word *sadutiyavihari.* It is the opposite of "living alone." But when the Buddha used this word, he did not mean that the monk was living with other people. He meant that a monk who is bound by any objects, even objects of consciousness, is actually living with those objects.

The Buddha added, "Indeed, Migajala, if a monk is bound by any fetter like this, even if he lives deep in the forest, in a deserted place without others, and without any outer disturbance, he still lives with another. Why? Because he still has not thrown off the fetters that bind him. Those fetters are the ones with whom he lives."

Buddha taught Migajala that a person who knows the better way to live alone is someone who lives at ease, not bound by the internal formations which are based on the objects of the six senses: form, sound, smell, taste, touch, and the objects of the mind.

The Buddha concluded, "Migajala, if a monk lives like this, even in the center of a village; with monks, nuns, or lay practitioners; among royalty, or high-ranking officials; or with those who practice another way, he is still someone who knows the better way to live alone. He can be said to be living alone because he has freed himself from all attachments."

The Bhaddekaratta gatha was composed by the Buddha to summarize what he had taught Thera and Migajala. The Buddha read this gatha to the monks in the Jetavana monastery and later commented on it for them. The opening paragraphs of the sutra depict the occasion on which the Sutra On Knowing the Better Way to Live Alone was delivered.

The people who were able to hear the Buddha that day were limited to the monks who were present in the Jetavana monastery. Because of the importance of the subject, monks and nuns living elsewhere gradually came to know about the "Knowing the Better Way to Live Alone" gatha. The God of the Forest Hot Springs Sutra tells us that at that time, the Buddha was staying in Rajagriha at the Venuvana monastery. The monk Samiddhi was residing in the nearby forest. One morning after bathing in the hot springs, Samiddhi was putting on his robe when a beautiful god appeared, prostrated before him, and asked him if he had ever heard and practiced the "Knowing the Better Way to Live Alone" gatha, saying, "Venerable Samiddhi, you should ask the Buddha to teach us this gatha so that we can put it into practice. I have heard that this gatha contains the deepest meaning of the Buddha's teachings, that it is the basis for the enlightened life, and that it can lead to awakened understanding and *nirvana*." After the god had spoken, he joined his palms and walked clockwise three times around the monk to show his respect.

The monk Samiddhi went to the Buddha. After prostrating to the Awakened One, he told about his encounter with the god and asked the Buddha to teach him the "Knowing the Better Way to Live Alone" gatha. Buddha asked Samiddhi if he knew who the god was. When Samiddhi replied that he did not, Buddha told him the god's name and that he came from the thirty-third heaven. Then Samiddhi and the monks who were present asked the Buddha again to teach them the gatha. Buddha recited it for them:

Do not pursue the past.
Do not lose yourself in the future. The past no longer is.
The future has not yet come. Looking deeply at life as it is in the
very here and now, the practitioner dwells
in stability and freedom. We must be diligent today.
To wait until tomorrow is too late.
Death comes unexpectedly.
How can we bargain with it? The sage calls a person
who dwells in mindfulness
night and day
"the one who knows
the better way to live alone."

After reciting the gatha, the Buddha left his seat and returned to his hut to meditate. The monks, including Samiddhi, wished to hear an explanation of it, so they went to the elder Kaccana, a senior disciple of the Buddha, recited the gatha to him, and asked if he would comment on it. The monk Kaccana was known to have many excellent qualities. He was often praised by the Buddha for his intelligence, and the monks thought he would be able to offer a penetrating explanation. At first Kaccana hesitated. He suggested that the monks go directly to the Buddha, so that the commentary was from the Teacher himself. But in the end, because the bhikkhus insisted, he agreed to explain the gatha to them. This elder's commentary is the essential content of The God of the Forest Hot Springs Sutra.

After offering his explanation of the gatha, the elder told the monks that if the opportunity presented itself, they should ask Buddha to explain it directly, because his own insight could never be as profound as the insight of the Awakened One.

The bhikkhus, including Samiddhi, did have another audience with the Buddha, and they told the Buddha the explanation of the "Knowing the Better Way to Live Alone" gatha that they had heard from Kaccana. The Buddha began by speaking in praise of the elder: "Excellent. Among my disciples there are those who grasp the meaning of the Dharma and understand its significance. If the teacher recites a gatha and does not have a chance to comment on it, then it is the disciples who must penetrate the meaning of the gatha and give a fuller explanation of the teaching. The Elder Kaccana is a senior bhikkhu. The commentary he gave you shows the true meaning of the gatha and is in accord with the truth of the way things are. You should use it and make it part of your practice."

This exchange took place in Rajagriha, the capital city of Magadha, on the right bank of the Ganges. The account which follows took place further north and west, in the town of Shravasti, the capital of the kingdom of Koshala, on the left bank of the Ganges. That account is given in the Shakyan Hermitage Sutra.

The Shakyan Hermitage had been built by members of the Shakyan clan in the hills not far from Shravasti. This hermitage also had the name "No Problems" or "At Peace." At that time, the bhikkhu Lomasakangiya was staying in the hermitage. One night shortly before daybreak, he stepped outside and spread out a cloth on one of the string cots under the trees. As soon as he began to sit on the cot in the lotus position, a very beautiful god appeared, prostrated before him, and asked if he knew the "Knowing the Better Way to Live Alone" gatha and if he had ever heard a commentary on it. The monk in turn asked the god the same question, and the god replied that he had heard the gatha but he had not yet had the chance to hear the commentary explaining the deep meaning of the gatha. The elder asked, "How is it that you have heard the gatha but have not yet heard the commentary?"

The god explained that at one time, when the Buddha was residing in Rajagriha, he had heard the Buddha recite the gatha, but the Buddha had given no commentary.

Then the god recited the gatha and advised the monk to go and ask the Buddha to explain it. The gatha in this sutra is identical to the one in The God of the Forest Hot Springs Sutra.

After that, the bhikkhu Lomasakangiya went to the Buddha and told him what had happened. At that time, the Buddha was staying in the Jetavana monastery in Shravasti. Having heard the account, the Buddha told Lomasakangiya that the name of the god who had appeared to him was Candana (Sandalwood) and that he came from the thirty-third heaven. Then bhikkhu Lomasakangiya requested the Buddha to explain the gatha.

That day, there were many bhikkhus present. The Buddha's commentary on the gatha forms the essence of the Shakyan Hermitage Sutra.*

Another sutra related to the Sutra on Knowing the Better Way to Live Alone is the Sutra Spoken by Ānanda.† The Buddha delivered this discourse at Shravasti. One night the Venerable Ānanda asked the monks to assemble in the main Dharma hall of the Jetavana monastery, and he recited and explained the "Knowing the Better Way to Live Alone" gatha. Early the next day, one of the bhikkhus went to see the Buddha and told him about Ānanda's Dharma talk. The sutra does not say that the bhikkhu expressed any lack of confidence in the Venerable Ānanda, but the sutra does say that after the Buddha heard about the Dharma talk, he sent the bhikkhu to invite Ānanda to join them.

When Ānanda arrived in the Buddha's room, the Buddha asked him, "Is it true that you recited and gave a talk on the gatha, 'Knowing the Better Way to Live Alone' last night?" Ānanda replied that it was true, and the Buddha asked, "Can you recite it for me and tell me your commentary on it?" After Ānanda recited the gatha and told the Buddha his

* *Madhyama Agama 167, equivalent to the Ānanda-Bhaddekaratta in the Pali Canon, Majjhima Nikāya 132.*

† *Madhyama Agama 166, which is the equivalent of the Lomasakangiya-Bhaddekaratta, number 134 in the Majjhima Nikāya.*

explanation of it, the Buddha asked Ānanda several more questions. The main part of the Sutra Spoken by Ānanda is comprised of the answers given by Ānanda to the Buddha's questions. When he heard Ānanda's answers, he praised him saying, "Excellent! Among my disciples there are those who have the insight to understand the essential significance of the teachings."

Buddha praised Ānanda in the way that he had praised Kaccana. On that day there were many bhikkhus present, among them the bhikkhu who had told the Buddha about Ānanda's Dharma talk. Perhaps the Buddha spoke those words to assure the monks that the Venerable Ānanda's grasp of the Dharma was as firm as Kaccana's and that the bhikkhus could make Ānanda's teachings a part of their practice.

Putting the Teachings of the Buddha into Practice

To live alone does not mean to reject the world and society. The Buddha said that living alone means living in the present moment, deeply observing what is happening. If we do that, we will not be dragged into the past or swept away into thoughts about the future. The Buddha said that if we cannot live in the present moment, even if we are alone in the deepest forest, we are not really alone. He said that if we are fully alive in the present moment, even if we are in a crowded urban area, we can still be said to be living alone.

It is important to practice in a community. A Vietnamese proverb goes: "Soup is to a meal what friends are to the practice." When we practice in a community, we can learn from its members, and take refuge in our communal practice. We need to discover the way of being alone in a practice community.

The monk Thera was part of a practice community, but he was determined to live alone. He believed in the idea of a solitary life, because he had at some time heard the Buddha praising the practice of living alone. So he kept his distance from everyone else. He begged for alms alone, he returned alone, he ate alone, and he meditated alone. He was like a drop of oil in a bowl of water, unable to mix with his fellow practitioners. The other monastics felt something was not right with his practice, and they expressed their concern to the Buddha.

The Buddha was very kind. He did not criticize Thera. He only said that Thera's way of living alone was not the best way of doing so. Because there were many other monks present at the time and they could benefit from the teaching, the Buddha took the opportunity to teach Thera that the better way of living alone is to associate with the other monastics, to learn from them and take refuge in them.

There were bhikkhus who were the opposite of Thera, who would always gather in small groups and fritter away their time chatting and joking. Their conversations were not about the teachings, and the Buddha frequently reprimanded them. There are stories throughout the sutras in which the Buddha advises or chides the bhikkhus who act in a noisy and undisciplined way, not knowing how to keep body and mind in check, not knowing how to spend their time usefully in practicing walking and sitting meditation and observing deeply things as they are in the present moment.*

When I first became a monk, my master gave me a copy of the book *The Admonitions and Encouraging Words of Master Guishan*. I will never forget the sentences in which Master Guishan reprimands practitioners who, after the midday meal, gather in small groups and talk about meaningless things. Guishan's words of advice have often come back to me and served as a reminder:

> When you receive food offered by donors, wouldn't it be better to meditate on the food than to think that as a monk you deserve to receive it? When you finish eating, if you sit around talking idly, it will increase everyone's suffering

* *In the Pali Canon, see the Nagita Sutta, Anguttara Nikāya chapters 5.30, 6.42, 8.86. In the Chinese Canon, see Samyukta Agama 1250 and 1251.*

> later on. How many lifetimes do you plan to chase after worldly matters without looking deeply at where your life is going? Time flies like an arrow, yet you are still attached to the pleasure of the offerings you receive, and you still think that money and possessions will provide you security. The Buddha taught his monks to be satisfied with just enough food, clothing, and shelter. Why would a monk or a nun spend so much time craving these things? By the time you wake up, your hair will be white. Listen to the wise ones. They did not become monks and nuns just to have some food to eat and a robe to wear.*

When we live in a practice community, there should always be at least one or two people who serve as role models. Sometimes we only need to watch them standing, walking, speaking, or smiling in mindfulness, and we feel steady in our own practice. The fact that we know "the better way to live alone" does not prevent us from enjoying and benefitting from the presence of such people. On the contrary, it is because we know "the better way to live alone" that we have the ability to observe them deeply and appreciate them.

To be in touch does not mean just to talk with the other person. When we are in touch with the blue sky, for example, the white clouds, the green willow, or the rose, we do not communicate with them only in words. We recognize and accept these things, and feel their warmth. Confidence

* *For the full text, see Thich Nhat Hanh,* Stepping Into Freedom *(Parallax Press, 1997).*

springs up in us, and we learn a lot from their presence. In this way we are able to profit from the third jewel, the practice community.

If we practice "the better way of living alone," and we spend most of our time quietly practicing walking and sitting meditation, our presence will make a real contribution to the community. Unlike the monk Thera or the monks who gather after meals to talk about things that are not important, every step we make adds to the quality and stability of the practice in the community. We are like Śāriputra, Kashyapa, Bhaddiya, or Kimbila—all students of the Buddha. Seeing us, the Buddha will be satisfied and smile. The Buddha knows that if every individual in the community knows how to live alone, the quality of life in the community will be excellent. When all the members of the community contribute to that quality, the community has a strong foundation, and many people can benefit from it. To live alone means to live in mindfulness. It does not mean to isolate oneself from society. If we know the better way to live alone, we can be in real touch with people and society, and we will know what to do and what not to do to be of help.

Awake and Alone

If we live in forgetfulness, if we lose ourselves in the past or in the future, if we allow ourselves to be tossed about by our desires, anger, and ignorance, we will not be able to live each moment of our life deeply. We will not be in contact with what is happening in the present moment, and our relations with others will become shallow and impoverished.

Some days we may feel hollow, exhausted, and joyless, not really our true selves. On such days, even if we try to be in touch with others, our efforts will be in vain. The more we try, the more we fail. When this happens, we should stop trying to be in touch with what is outside of ourselves and come back to being in touch with ourselves. We should "be alone." This is a time to practice conscious breathing, observing deeply what is going on inside and around us. We can accept all the phenomena we observe, say hello to them, and smile at them. We do well to do simple things, like walking or sitting meditation, washing our clothes, cleaning the floor, making tea, and cleaning the bathroom in mindfulness. If we do these things, we will restore the richness of our spiritual life.

The Buddha was someone who lived an awakened life, dwelling constantly in the present moment in a relaxed and steady way. There was always a richness about him—a richness of freedom, joy, understanding, and love. Whether he was seated on a rocky crag of Vulture Peak, in the shade of the bamboo groves of Venuvana monastery, or under the thatched roof of his hut in Jetavana, Buddha was Buddha, unagitated, content, and of few words. Everyone could see that his presence contributed greatly to the harmony and stability of the community. The monks and nuns were affected just by knowing he was nearby. Many students of the Buddha, including hundreds of senior disciples, inspired similar confidence in those who observed them. King Prasenajit of

Koshala once told the Buddha that what gave him so much confidence in the Buddha was the unhurried, calm, and joyful way of life of the monks and nuns who were practicing under his guidance.

If we live in mindfulness, we are no longer poor, because our practice of living in the present moment makes us rich in joy, peace, understanding, and love. Even when we encounter someone poor in spirit, we can look deeply and discover that person's rich layers.

When we watch a documentary or read a book or look at someone's painting or sculpture, if we are already poor in heart and mind, and weak in mindfulness, what we are reading or looking at may irritate us and make us feel even more poor. But if we are rich in mindfulness, we will discover what lies in the depths of that art. We may be able to see deeply into the inner world of the person who made it. Looking with the eyes of an art critic, we can see things that most people do not see, and even a bad movie or book or sculpture can teach us. Maintaining full awareness of each detail of the present moment, we are able to profit from it. This is the better way to live alone.

Tied Up Inside

The "Knowing the Better Way To Live Alone" gatha begins with the line: "Do not pursue the past." To "pursue the past" means to regret what has already come and gone. We regret the loss of the beautiful things of the past which we can no longer find in the present. Buddha commented on this line as follows: "When someone thinks how their body was in the past, how their feelings were in the past, how their perceptions were in the past, how their mental formations were in the past, how their consciousness was in the past, when they think like that and give rise to a mind which is enslaved by those things which belong to the past, then that person is pursuing the past."

Buddha taught that we should not pursue the past "because the past no longer is." When we are lost in thoughts about the past, we lose the present. Life exists only in the present moment. To lose the present is to lose life. The Buddha's meaning is very clear: we must say goodbye to the past so that we may return to the present. To return to the present is to be in touch with life.

What dynamics in our consciousness compel us to go back and live with the images of the past? These forces are made up of internal formations (Sanskrit: *samyojana*), mental formations which arise in us and bind us. Things we see, hear, smell, taste, touch, imagine, or think can all give rise to internal formations—desire, irritation, anger, confusion, fear, anxiety, suspicion, and so on. Internal formations are present in the depths of the consciousness of each of us.

Internal formations influence our consciousness and our everyday behavior. They cause us to think, say, and do things that we may not even be aware of. Because they compel us in this way, they are also called fetters, because they bind us to acting in certain ways.

The commentaries usually mention nine kinds of internal formations: desire, hatred, pride, ignorance, stubborn views, attachment, doubt, jealousy, and selfishness. Among these, the fundamental internal formation is ignorance, the lack of clear seeing. Ignorance is the raw material out of which the other internal formations are made. Although there are nine internal formations, because "desire" is always listed first, it is often used to represent all the internal formations. In the Kaccana-Bhaddekaratta, the monk Kaccana explains:

> My friends, what is meant by dwelling in the past? Someone thinks, "In the past my eyes were like that and the form (with which my eyes were in contact) was like that," and thinking like this, they are bound by desire. Bound by desire, there is a feeling of longing. This feeling of longing keeps them dwelling in the past.

Kaccana's commentary could make us think that the only internal formation holding one in the past is desire. But when Kaccana refers to "desire," he is using it to represent all the internal formations—hatred, doubt, jealousy, and so forth. All of these tie us and hold us back in the past.

Sometimes we only have to hear the name of someone who has wronged us in the past, and our internal formations from that time automatically take us back into the past, and we relive the suffering. The past is the home ground of both painful and happy memories. Being absorbed in the past is a way of being dead to the present moment. It is not easy to drop the past and return to living in the present. When we try to do it, we have to resist the force of the internal formations in us. We have to learn to transform our internal formations, so that we will be free to be attentive to the present moment.

Standing Firmly

The present contains the past. When we understand how our internal formations cause conflicts in us, we can see how the past is in the present moment, and we will no longer be overwhelmed by the past. When the Buddha said, "Do not pursue the past," he was telling us not to be overwhelmed by the past. He did not mean that we should stop looking at the past in order to observe it deeply. When we review the past and observe it deeply, if we are standing firmly in the present, we are not overwhelmed by it. The materials of the past which make up the present become clear when they express themselves in the present. We can learn from them. If we observe these materials deeply, we can arrive at a new understanding of them. That is called "looking again at something old in order to learn something new."

If we know that the past also lies in the present, we understand that we are able to change the past by transforming the present. The ghosts of the past, which follow us into the present, also belong to the present moment. To observe them deeply, recognize their nature, and transform them, is to transform the past. The ghosts of the past are very real. They are the internal formations in us, which are sometimes quietly asleep, while at other times they awaken suddenly and forcefully. There is the Sanskrit term *anusaya*. *Anu* means "along with." *Saya* means "lying down." We could translate anusaya as "latent tendency." The internal formations continue to be with us, but they are lying asleep in the depths of our consciousness. We call them ghosts, but they are present in a very real way. According to the Vijñānavāda school of Buddhism, anusaya are seeds which lie in everyone's subconscious (*ālāya*). An important part of the work of observation meditation is to be able to recognize the anusaya when they manifest, observe them deeply, and transform them.

Future Ghosts

Sometimes, because the present is so difficult, we give our attention to the future, hoping that the situation will improve in the future. Imagining the future will be better, we are better able to accept the suffering and hardship of the present. But at other times, thinking about the future may cause us a lot of fear and anxiety, and yet we cannot stop doing it. The reason we continue to think about the future, even when we do not want to, is due to the presence of internal formations. Although not yet here, the future is already producing ghosts which haunt us. In fact, these ghosts are not produced by the future or the past. It is our consciousness which creates them. The past and the future are creations of our consciousness.

The energies behind our thinking about the future are our hopes, dreams, and anxieties. Our hopes can be the result of our sufferings and failures. Because the present does not bring us happiness, we allow our minds to travel into the future. We hope that in the future, the situation will be brighter: "When someone considers how their body will be in the future, how their feelings will be in the future, how their mental formations will be in the future, how their consciousness will be in the future. . . ." Thinking in this way can give us the courage to accept failure and suffering in the present. The poet Tru Vu said that the future is the vitamin for the present. Hope brings us back some of the joys of life that we have lost.

We all know that hope is necessary for life. But according to Buddhism, hope can be an obstacle. If we invest our mind in the future, we will not have enough mental energy to face and transform the present. Naturally we have the right to make plans for the future, but making plans for the future does not mean to be being swept away by daydreams. While we are making plans, our feet are firmly planted in the present. We can only build the future from the raw materials of the present.

The essential teaching of Buddhism is to be free of all desire for the future in order to come back with all our heart and mind into the present. To realize awakening means to arrive at a deep and full insight into reality, which is in the present moment. In order to return to the present and to be face to face with what is happening, we must look deeply into the heart of what is and experience its true nature. When we do so, we experience the deep understanding which can release us from suffering and darkness.

According to Buddhism, hell, paradise, *samsara,* and *nirvana* are all here in the present moment. To return to the present moment is to discover life and to realize the truth. All the Awakened Ones of the past have come to Awakening in the present moment. All the Awakened Ones of the present and the future will realize the fruit of Awakening in the present also. Only the present moment is real: "The past no longer is, and the future has not yet come."

If we do not stand firmly in the present moment, we may feel ungrounded when we look at the future. We may think that in the future we will be alone, with no place of refuge and no one to help us. "When someone considers how their body will be in the future, how their feelings will be in the future, how their mental formations will be in the future, how their consciousness will be in the future ...." Such concerns about the future bring about unease, anxiety, and fear, and do not help us at all in taking care of the present moment. They just make our way of dealing with the present weak and confused. There is a Confucian saying that a person who does not know how to plan for the distant future will be troubled and perplexed by the near future. This is meant to remind us to care for the future, but not to be anxious and fearful about it. The best way of preparing for the future is to take good care of the present, because we know that if the present is made up of the past, then the future will be made up of the present. All we need to be responsible for is the present moment. Only the present is within our reach. To care for the present is to care for the future.

Smiling Within

When we think about the past, feelings of regret or shame may arise. When we think about the future, feelings of desire or fear may come up. But all of these feelings arise in the present moment, and they all affect the present moment. Most of the time, their effect does not contribute to our happiness or joy. We have to learn how to face these feelings. The main thing we need to remember is that the past and the future are both in the present, and if we take hold of the present moment, then we also transform the past and the future.

How can we transform the past? In the past we may have said or done something destructive or harmful, and now we regret it. According to Buddhist psychology, regret is an "indeterminate emotion." This means that it can be either constructive or destructive. When we know that something we have said or done has caused harm, we may give rise to a mind of repentance, vowing that in the future we will not repeat the same mistake. In this case, our feeling of regret has a wholesome effect. If, on the other hand, the feeling of regret continues to disturb us, making it impossible for us to concentrate on anything else, taking all the peace and joy out of our lives, then that feeling of regret has an unwholesome effect.

When regret becomes unwholesome, we should first distinguish whether the cause was based on something we did or said, or on something we failed to do or say. If in the past, we said or did something destructive, we can call that an "error of commission." We did or said something with a lack of mindfulness, and it caused harm. Sometimes we commit an "error of omission." We did harm by not saying or doing what needed to be said or done, and that brought us regret and sorrow. Our lack of mindfulness was there, and its results are still present. Our pain, shame, and regret are an important part of that result. If we observe the present deeply and take hold of it, we can transform it. We do so by means of mindfulness, determination, and correct actions and speech. All these come about in the present moment. When we transform the present in this way, we also transform the past, and at the same time, we build the future.

If we say that all is lost, everything is destroyed, or the suffering has already happened, we do not see that the past has become the present. Of course, the suffering has already been caused and the wound of that suffering can touch our very soul, but instead of lamenting about or suffering from what we have done in the past, we should take hold of the present and transform it. The traces of a bad drought can only be erased by a bountiful rainfall, and rain can only fall in the present moment.

Buddhist repentance is based on the understanding that wrongdoing originates in the mind. There is a gatha of repentance:

> *All wrongdoing arises from the mind.*
> *If mind is purified, what trace of wrong is left?*
> *After repentance, my heart is light*
> *like the white clouds that have always floated over the ancient forest in freedom.*

Because of our lack of mindfulness, because our mind was obscured by desire, anger, and jealousy, we acted wrongly. That is what is meant by "All wrongdoing arises from the mind." But if the wrongdoing arose from our mind, it can also be transformed within our mind. If our mind is transformed, then the objects perceived by our mind will also be transformed. Such transformation is available if we know how to return to the present moment. Once we have transformed our mind, our heart will be as light as a floating cloud, and we become a source of peace and joy for ourselves and others. Yesterday, perhaps out of foolishness or anger, we said something which made our mother sad. But today our mind is transformed and our heart light, and we can see our mother smiling at us, even if she is no longer alive. If we can smile within ourselves, our mother can also smile with us.

If we can transform the past, we can also transform the future. Our anxieties and fears for the future make the present dark. There is no doubt that the future will be black too, because we know that the future is made up of the present. Taking care of the present is the best way to take care of the future. Sometimes, because we are so concerned about what will happen the next day, we toss and turn all night, unable to sleep. We worry that if we cannot sleep during the night, we will be tired the next day and unable to perform to the best of our ability. The more we worry, the more difficult it is for us to sleep. Our worries and fears for the future destroy the present. But if we stop thinking about tomorrow and just stay in bed and follow our breathing, really enjoying the opportunity we have to rest, not only will we savor the moments of peace and joy under the warm blankets, but we will fall asleep quite easily and naturally. That kind of sleep is a big help for making the next day a success.

When we hear that the forests of our planet are diseased and dying so rapidly, we may feel anxious. We are concerned for the future, because we are aware of what is happening in the present moment. Our awareness can motivate us to do something to halt the destruction of our environment. Obviously, our concern for the future is different from worry and anxiety which only drain us. We have to know how to enjoy the presence of beautiful, healthy trees in order to be able to do something to protect and preserve them.

When we throw a banana peel into the compost heap, if we are mindful, we know that the peel will become compost and be reborn as a tomato or as lettuce in just a few months. But when we throw a plastic bag into the garbage, thanks to our awareness, we know that a plastic bag will not become a tomato or a salad very quickly. Some kinds of garbage need four or five hundred years to decompose. Nuclear waste needs a quarter of a million years before it stops being harmful and returns to the soil. Living in the present moment in an awakened way, looking after the present moment with all our heart, we will not do things which destroy the future. That is the most concrete way to do what is constructive for the future.

In our everyday life, we may also produce poisons for our minds, and these poisons destroy not only us but also those who live with us, in the present and in the future too. Buddhism talks about three poisons: desire, hatred, and ignorance. In addition, there are other poisons whose capacity to do harm is very great: jealousy, prejudice, pride, suspicion, and obstinacy.

In our day-to-day relationships with ourselves, others, and our environment, any or all of these poisons can manifest, blaze up, and destroy our peace and joy, as well as the peace and joy of those around us. These poisons can linger and pollute our minds, causing bitter consequences in the future. So to live in the present moment is also to accept and face these poisons as they arise, manifest, and return to the unconscious, and to practice observation meditation in order to transform them. This is a Buddhist practice. To live in the present is also to see the wonderful and wholesome things in order to nourish and protect them. Happiness is the direct result of facing things and being in touch. That happiness is the material from which a beautiful future is constructed.

Life Is a Path

To return to the present is to be in contact with life. Life can be found only in the present moment, because "the past no longer is" and "the future has not yet come." Buddhahood, liberation, awakening, peace, joy, and happiness can only be found in the present moment. Our appointment with life is in the present moment. The place of our appointment is right here, in this very place.

According to the Avatamsaka Sutra, time and space are not separate. Time is made up of space, and space is made up of time. When we speak about spring, we usually think of time, but spring is also space. When it is spring in Europe, it is winter in Australia.

When we have a tea mediation, those who attend breathe in and out and recite the following gatha together before taking the first sip of tea:

This cup of tea in my two hands—
mindfulness is held uprightly.
My mind and body dwell
in the very here and now.

When we drink tea in mindfulness, we practice coming back to the present moment to live our life right here. When our mind and our body are fully in the present moment, then the steaming cup of tea appears clearly to us. We know it is a wonderful aspect of existence. At that time we are really in contact with the cup of tea. It is only at times like this that life is really present.

Peace, joy, liberation, awakening, happiness, Buddhahood, the source—everything we long for and seek after can only be found in the present moment. To abandon the present moment in order to look for these things in the future is to throw away the substance and hold on to the shadow. In Buddhism, aimlessness (*apraṇihitā*) is taught as a way to help the practitioner stop pursuing the future and return wholly to the present. Aimlessness is sometimes called wishlessness, and it is one of the "three doors of liberation." (The other two are emptiness and signlessness.) To be able to stop pursuing the future allows us to realize that all the wonderful things we seek are present in us, in the present moment. Life is not a particular place or a destination. Life is a path. To practice walking meditation is to go without needing to arrive. Every step can bring us peace, joy, and liberation. That is why we walk in the spirit of aimlessness. There is no way to liberation, peace, and joy; peace and joy are themselves the way. Our appointment with the Buddha, with liberation, with happiness, is here and now. We should not miss this appointment.

Buddhism teaches a way of breathing which gives us the capacity of making body and mind one in order to be face to face with life. This is called "oneness of body and mind." That is why every meditator begins by practicing the Sutra on the Full Awareness of Breathing (Ānāpānasati Sutta).

But to come back to the present does not mean to be carried away by what is happening in the present. The sutra teaches us to observe life deeply and be in touch with the present moment, and see all the sufferings and the wonders of the present. Yet we must do so in mindfulness, maintaining a high degree of awareness in order not to be carried away by, or caught in, desire for or aversion to what is happening in the present.

> *Looking deeply at life as it is*
> *in the very here and now,*
> *the practitioner dwells*
> *in stability and freedom.*

"Stability and freedom" refer to the contentment and tranquility of not being carried away by anything whatsoever. Stability and ease are two characteristics of nirvana. The Pali version of this verse uses two terms, *asaṅkuppaṁ* and *asaṁhīraṁ*. Asaṅkuppaṁ means "unwavering, unshakable, immovable, unexcitable." Sanghadeva, the monk and translator of the Madhyama Agama, translates it as "firm and unwavering." The monk Dharmapala translates it as "stable." Asaṁhīraṁ means, literally, "not folded together, not restrained, not collected, not carried away by anything." Sanghadeva translated asaṁhīraṁ into Chinese as "non-existing" (*wu yu*), which is not exact. Dharmapala, in The Elder Sutra, translated asaṁhīraṁ as "not fettered." "Fettered" here means "imprisoned." So "not fettered" means "not caught" or "in freedom."

Being in contact with life in the present moment, we observe deeply what is. Then we are able to see the impermanent and selfless nature of all that is. Impermanence and selflessness are not negative aspects of life but the very foundations on which life is built. Impermanence is the constant transformation of things. Without impermanence, there can be no life. Selflessness is the interdependent nature of all things. Without interdependence, nothing could exist. Without the sun, the clouds, and the Earth, the tulip could not be. We often feel sad about the impermanence and selflessness of life, because we forget that without impermanence and selflessness, life cannot be. To be aware of impermanence and selflessness does not take away the joy of being alive. On the contrary, it adds healthiness, stability, and freedom. It is because people cannot see the impermanent and selfless nature of things that they suffer. They take what is impermanent as permanent and what is selfless as having a self.

Looking deeply into a rose, we can see its impermanent nature quite clearly. At the same time, we can see its beauty and value its preciousness. Because we perceive its fragile and impermanent nature, we may see that flower as even more beautiful and precious. The more fragile something is, the more beautiful and precious it is—for example, a rainbow, a sunset, a cereus cactus flowering by night, a falling star. Looking at the sun rising over Vulture Peak, at the town of Vaishali, at a field of ripe, golden rice, the Buddha saw their beauty and told Ānanda so.

Seeing deeply the impermanent nature of those beautiful things, their transformation and disappearance, the Buddha did not suffer or despair. We, too, by observing deeply and seeing impermanence and selflessness in all that is, can overcome despair and suffering and experience the preciousness of the miracles of everyday life—a glass of clear water, a cool breeze, a step taken in ease and freedom. These are wonderful things, although they are impermanent and selfless.

Life is suffering, but it is also wonderful. Sickness, old age, death, accidents, starvation, unemployment, and natural disasters cannot be avoided in life. But, if our understanding is deep and our mind free, we can accept these things with tranquility, and the suffering will already be greatly lessened. This is not to say we should close our eyes before suffering. By being in contact with suffering, we give rise to and nourish our natural love and compassion. Suffering becomes the element which nourishes our love and compassion, and so we are not afraid of it. When our heart is filled with love and compassion, we will act in ways to help relieve the suffering of others.

If the human species has been able to make any progress, it is because of our heart of love and compassion. We need to learn from compassionate beings how to develop the practice of deep observation for the sake of others. Then others will be able to learn from us the way to live in the present and see the impermanent and selfless nature of all that is. This insight will lighten suffering.

Fear of the unexpected leads many people to live a constricted and anxious life. No one can know in advance the misfortunes which may happen to us and our loved ones, but if we learn to live in an awakened way, living deeply every moment of our life, treating those who are close to us with gentleness and understanding, then we will have nothing to regret when something happens to us or to them. Living in the present moment, we are able to be in touch with life's wonderful, refreshing, and health-giving phenomena, which allow us to heal the wounds in ourselves. Every day we become more wonderful, fresh, and healthy.

Peace, Freedom, and Joy

To practice a life of deep observation according to the teachings of the Buddha is to have a life of peace, freedom, and joy, and to realize complete liberation. The "Knowing the Better Way to Live Alone" gatha reminds us that we cannot avoid death and advises us to be diligent in the practice today, for tomorrow it will be too late. Death comes unexpectedly, and there is no way to bargain with it. If we live observing everything deeply in the present moment, we learn to live in peace and joy with freedom and stability. If we continue to practice diligently in this way, peace, joy, and stability will grow every day until we realize complete liberation. When there is complete liberation, death can no longer harm us.

A life like this will bring joy to our dear ones and others. The material of stability and release is also the element of liberation. Liberation is the fruit of deep observation which leads to the realization of the impermanent and selfless nature of all that is. By observing at a deep level, we can defeat death, because the observation of impermanence can lead us to transcend the boundaries of birth and death. When we look at all that is in the universe and all those dear to us, we see that there is nothing eternal and unchanging that we can call "I" or "self."

Transcending Birth and Death

We often think that birth means that what did not exist comes into existence, and that death means that which exists ceases to exist. When we look deeply at things, we see that this idea about birth and death is mistaken in many respects. No phenomenon whatsoever can come into existence out of nothing, and no phenomenon which exists can become nothing. Things are ceaselessly transforming. The cloud does not die; it only becomes rain. The rain is not born; it is only the transformation and continuation of the cloud. Leaves, a pair of shoes, joy, and sorrow all conform to this principle of no-birth and no-death. To think that after death we no longer exist is a narrow view which in Buddhism is called the "nihilistic view." The narrow view that after death we continue to exist without changing is called the "view of permanence." Reality transcends both permanence and annihilation.

The Buddha taught us to look directly into the elements which combine together to constitute our body, in order to see the nature of these elements and transcend the idea of "self"—whether it is the idea of a permanent, indestructible self, or the idea of a self subject to complete annihilation after we die. The sutra says: "Someone who studies and learns about the Awakened One, the teachings of love and understanding, and the community which lives in harmony and awareness, who knows about noble teachers and their teachings, practices these teachings, and does not think, 'This body is myself, I am this body; these feelings are myself, I am these feelings; this perception is myself, I am this perception; this mental formation is myself, I am this mental formation; this consciousness is myself, I am this consciousness,' then that person does not go back to the past, does not think ahead to the future, and is not being swept away by the present."

The five elements which combine together to become the thing we call self are form (the body), feelings, perceptions, mental formations, and consciousness. If we look penetratingly into the substance of these elements and see their impermanent and interdependent nature, we naturally see that there is no entity we can call "self." All five elements are constantly transforming. They are never born and never die. There is no element that goes from nothingness into existence, nor any element which goes from existence into nothingness. The thing which we think of as "I" is not born and does not die. We do not identify "I" with the body, whether that body is developing or degenerating, nor with the feelings which change at every moment. Similarly, we do not identify with our perceptions and our consciousness. We are not bound or limited by these five elements. We see that if these elements really are not born or destroyed, then we need no longer be oppressed by death. This insight enables us to transcend birth and death.

When the sutra refers to someone who "practices according to the teachings of the Noble Ones," it means someone who lives in the present and observes deeply in order to see life's impermanent and selfless nature. The Buddha taught that "we must practice diligently today, for tomorrow will be too late; death comes unexpectedly and there is no bargaining with it." Observing deeply, we can realize the birthless and deathless nature of things, and there is nothing more which can frighten us, not even death. We directly overcome birth and death when, by deep observation and realization of impermanence and selflessness, we pierce through false ideas about the nature of existence. Once we overcome death, we no longer need to "bargain with death." We can smile, take the hand of death, and go for a walk together.

The life called the "brahma-faring life" of a monk or a nun can lead to the realization of the birthless and deathless nature of all that is. That realization is the substance of liberation. That is why in the Kaccana-Bhaddekaratta Sutra it is emphasized that the practice of living alone is the basis of the brahma-faring life of a monk or a nun. It is also the basis of life for all of us.

Appendix

The Bhaddekaratta Gatha in Other Sutras

Knowing the better way to live alone shines light on the essence of living in an awakened way as taught by the Buddha. The sutra teaches us to let go of the past and the future, and to live mindfully in order to look deeply and discover the true nature of all that is taking place in the present moment.

The Bhaddekaratta Gatha in the Pali Canon

The Bhaddekaratta gatha became well known and is found in many other sutras in both the Pali Canon and the Chinese Canon.

In the Pali Canon, I have come across four suttas with the "Bhaddekaratta" gatha, all in the Majjhima Nikāya. The first is the Bhaddekaratta Sutta (number 131). The second is the Ānanda-Bhaddekaratta Sutta (number 132), which is the equivalent of the Sutra Spoken by Ānanda. The third is the Mahakaccana-Bhaddekaratta Sutta (number 133), equivalent to The God of the Forest Hot Springs Sutra. The fourth is the

Lomasakangiya-Bhaddekaratta Sutta (M134), equivalent to the Shakyan Hermitage Sutra.

Besides the four Pali suttas and Chinese sutras mentioned above, the subject of living alone is referred to in many other places in the canons, in detail in the Theranamo and the Migajala sutras, although the Bhaddekaratta gatha is not specifically quoted.

The terms *ekavihari* (one who lives alone) and *sadutiyavihari* (one who lives with another) in the Migajala Sutta are easy to understand and accept. But the term *bhaddekaratta* is difficult to translate. Dharmanandi, who translated the Samyukta Agama into Chinese, did not understand this compound word, so he just transcribed it into Chinese characters and used it as the title of the gatha.*

A number of Buddhist masters of the Southern Tradition understand *ekaratta* as "one night" and translate Bhaddekaratta as "A Good Night for Meditation." Judging from the content of the sutra, I believe this translation is not correct. *Bhadda* means "good" or "ideal." *Eka* means "one" or "alone." *Ratta* means "to like." The contemporary Buddhist scholar Bhikkhu Ñanananda translates the title as "The Ideal Lover of Solitude." After much reflection, I think that "Knowing

* *Master Dharmapala translated* bhaddekaratta *as* xian shan. Xian *means "virtuous" or "able," and* shan *means "good," "good at," or "skillful." These two words translate* bhadda *and* ratta. *But the part* eka, *"alone," which lies between badha and ratta, has been overlooked, although it is fundamental to the meaning of the compound.*

the Better Way to Live Alone" is closer to the original meaning of the sutra.

The Bhaddekaratta Gatha in the Chinese Canon

In the Madhyama Agama there are three sutras which quote this gatha. The first is The God of the Forest Hot Springs Sutra (number 165), in which the poem is quoted four times. The second is The Shakyan Hermitage Sutra (number 166), in which the gatha is quoted three times. The third sutra is the Sutra Spoken by Ānanda (number 167), in which the gatha is quoted once. The following is the translation of the gatha as it appears in the three sutras:

Do not think of the past.
Do not worry about the future.
Things of the past have died.
The future has not arrived.
What is happening in the present
should be observed deeply.
The Wise Ones live according to this
and dwell in stability and freedom.
If one practices the teachings
of the Wise Ones,
why should one be afraid of death?
If we do not understand this,
there is no way to avoid
the great pain of the final danger.

To practice diligently day and night,
one should regularly recite
the Bhaddekaratta Gatha.

The following Bhaddekaratta Gatha is seen in the translation of the Great Reverence Sutra, which is no. 77 in the Taisho Revised Tripitaka.

Not thinking about the past,
not seeking something in the future—
the past has already died,
the future is not in our hands—
we should observe deeply
and contemplate
what is in the present moment.
The person who constantly practices
the way of the wise ones
has awakened understanding.
Diligently practicing,
without wavering, and
released from care,
what does he fear at the time of death?
If he does not practice diligently,
how can he overcome death and its armies?
Truly we should practice
according to this wonderful gatha.

About Thích Nhất Hạnh: Zen Master, Poet, and Activist

Thích Nhất Hạnh is considered one of the most influential teachers of Buddhism and a leading spokesperson for the Buddhist peace movement. He was a lifelong advocate for peace, human rights, and social justice. In all his teachings, Thích Nhất Hạnh places a high value on relating ancient wisdom to everyday life. "There is no enlightenment outside of everyday life," he says. Being present in the moment is what will bring us happiness. By bringing one's body and mind together in the present moment, we can experience peace and a unity with humanity and with all of life.

Thích Nhất Hạnh was born Nguyen Xuan Bao in 1926 in Central Vietnam during the harsh French colonial rule. At the age of sixteen, he entered the Zen monastery, Tu Hieu, just outside Hue, and began his training as a novice monk. After finishing his monastic training, Thích Nhất Hạnh went to Saigon, where he became the editor of *Vietnamese Buddhism*, a journal that was inspirational for young Buddhists and peace activists.

In 1954, Vietnam was divided into two countries and, with support from the United States, the Diệm regime was established in the south. This was the beginning of the US occupation and war.

In 1961, Thích Nhất Hạnh travelled to the United States on a scholarship to study comparative religion at Princeton Theological Seminary and the following year went on to teach and research Buddhism at Union Theological Seminary in New York City, then part of Columbia University. In 1964, he returned to Saigon where he founded the School of Youth for Social Service (SYSS), an example of what he would come to call "engaged Buddhism." The SYSS trained dedicated young monks, nuns, and laypeople as social workers to bring relief to people during the war. They helped rebuild villages and relocate refugees, and they provided food, education, medical and legal assistance, and spiritual support to people whose lives had been shattered by the war. Many SYSS students were injured or killed.

In 1966, Nhat Hanh founded the Tiếp Hiện Order, the Order of Interbeing. The order dedicates itself to the practice of Buddhism, mindfulness, social responsibility, and nonviolence. Two years later, Nhat Hanh traveled to the United States to inform people of the effects of the war and to call for peace. When word of his efforts reached Vietnam, he was refused permission to return home and he ultimately was granted asylum in France.

In the 1960s and early 1970s, he represented Vietnam's Buddhist Peace Delegation at the Paris peace talks between the United States and North Vietnam, where he gave voice to the great desire of ordinary Vietnamese people for peace and an end to the war. With the signing of the peace agreement and the end of the war in 1975, he had hoped to return home.

But the new Vietnamese government still considered him an enemy because he hadn't taken sides during the war, and so he was forced to remain in exile.

In 1982, Nhat Hanh founded Plum Village in southwest France, the first of many mindfulness practice centers around the world, where monks, nuns, and laypeople from many countries live together year-round as a sangha, or spiritual family. Living together, the community focuses on being the peace they would like to see in the world. Plum Village practice centers also welcome lay practitioners and families for stays of a week or more, bringing together people from all over the world. Palestinians and Israelis come together at Plum Village each year for special retreats. Many US veterans of the Vietnam War have also come to Plum Village or attended a retreat and discovered peace and resolution.

In January 2005, for the first time in thirty-nine years, Nhat Hanh was allowed to return for a three-month visit to Vietnam. During that trip he gave teachings, met with old friends and colleagues as well as government leaders, and introduced Plum Village practices at a number of monasteries. This was followed by two more trips to Vietnam in 2007 and 2008. In 2014 he experienced a severe brain hemorrhage that left him unable to speak. Returning in 2018 to his root temple, Từ Hiếu in Vietnam, he continued to connect people around the world to the practice of mindfulness through his loving interactions until his death on January 22, 2022.

Thích Nhất Hạnh's legacy continues to grow through the many practice centers and sanghas in the Plum Village tradition that can now be found around the world, as well as in institutions such as the Thích Nhất Hạnh Center for Mindfulness in Public Health at Harvard University, which was opened in 2023.

Monastics and visitors practice the art of mindful living in the tradition of Thich Nhat Hanh at our mindfulness practice centers around the world. To reach any of these communities, or for information about how individuals, couples, and families can join in a retreat, please contact:

PLUM VILLAGE
24240 Thénac, France
plumvillage.org

LA MAISON DE L'INSPIR
77510 Villeneuve-sur-Bellot, France
maisondelinspir.org

HEALING SPRING MONASTERY
77510 Verdelot, France
healingspringmonastery.org

MAGNOLIA GROVE MONASTERY
Batesville, MS 38606, USA
magnoliagrovemonastery.org

BLUE CLIFF MONASTERY
Pine Bush, NY 12566, USA
bluecliffmonastery.org

DEER PARK MONASTERY
Escondido, CA 92026, USA
deerparkmonastery.org

EUROPEAN INSTITUTE OF APPLIED BUDDHISM
D-51545 Waldbröl, Germany
eiab.eu

THAILAND PLUM VILLAGE
Nakhon Ratchasima
30130 Thailand
thaiplumvillage.org

ASIAN INSTITUTE OF APPLIED BUDDHISM
Lantau Island, Hong Kong
pvfhk.org

STREAM ENTERING MONASTERY
Porcupine Ridge, Victoria 3461
Australia
nhapluu.org

MOUNTAIN SPRING MONASTERY
Bilpin, NSW 2758, Australia
mountainspringmonastery.org

For more information visit: *plumvillage.org*
To find an online sangha visit: *plumline.org*
For more resources, try the Plum Village app: *plumvillage.app*
Social media: *@thichnhathanh @plumvillagefrance*

THICH NHAT HANH FOUNDATION

planting seeds of Compassion

THE THICH NHAT HANH FOUNDATION works to continue the mindful teachings and practices of Zen Master Thich Nhat Hanh in order to foster peace and transform suffering in all people, animals, plants, and our planet. Through donations to the Foundation, thousands of generous supporters ensure the continuation of Thich Nhat Hanh's vision and help care for practice centers and monastics around the world. Your gifts help bring transformative practices to people who otherwise could not access them and support local mindfulness initiatives that ease suffering and cultivate joy.

By becoming a supporter, you join thousands of others committed to learning about, embodying, and sharing the life-changing practices of mindfulness, loving speech, deep listening, and compassion for oneself, each other, and the world.

For more information on how you can help spread Thich Nhat Hanh's teachings and practices globally, and to subscribe to our newsletters offering teachings, news, and information about retreats, please visit tnhf.org.

Parallax Press

PARALLAX PRESS, a nonprofit publisher founded by Zen Master Thich Nhat Hanh, publishes books and media on the art of mindful living and Engaged Buddhism. We are committed to offering teachings that help transform suffering and injustice. Our aspiration is to contribute to collective insight and awakening, bringing about a more joyful, healthy, and compassionate society.

View our entire library at parallax.org.

the mindfulness bell

THE MINDFULNESS BELL is a journal of the art of mindful living in the Plum Village tradition of Thich Nhat Hanh. To subscribe or to see the worldwide directory of Sanghas (local mindfulness groups), visit mindfulnessbell.org.